KHUSHU
IN THE
PRAYER

SHAYKH ʿABDULLĀH BIN JĀR ALLĀH ĀLI JĀR
ALLĀH

© Maktabatulirshad Publications, USA

ISBN: 978-1-6841-9022-5

First Edition: Muharram 1437 A.H. / October 2016 C.E.

Cover Design: Maktabatulirshad Publications

Translation by Muhiydīn as-Somali
Revision & Editing by ʿAbdullāh Omrān

Typesetting & formatting by Abū Sulaymān Muḥammad ʿAbdul-ʿAẓīm Ibn Joshua Baker

Subject: Fiqh

Website: www.maktabatulirshad.com
E-mail: info@maktabatulirshad.com

ATTENTION IN ṢALĀH, ATTENTIVENESS OF THE HEART, AND TREATING DISTRACTIONS

All praise belongs to Allāh. He whom made Ṣalāh a pillar of the religion and a strong connection between Allāh and His believing servants. Peace and blessings be upon Muhammad, the Trustworthy, his family, and all his Companions.

As to what follows:

Khushu' is tranquility through peace and humility along with uprightness, as Allāh, the Most High says:

$$ \text{﴿ قَدْ أَفْلَحَ ٱلْمُؤْمِنُونَ ۝ ٱلَّذِينَ هُمْ فِى صَلَاتِهِمْ خَٰشِعُونَ ۝ ﴾} $$

"Successful indeed are the believers. Those who offer their *Ṣalāt* (prayers) with all solemnity and full submissiveness."

." [*Sūrah al-Mu'minūn* 23:1-2]

Meaning, indeed this is victory and happiness for the believers who perform Ṣalāh. As some of their traits are **"Those who offer their *Ṣalāh* (prayers) with all solemnity and full submissiveness."**

Al-Khushu' in Ṣalāh: Presence of the heart therein before Allāh, the Most High, in love and honor, fearing His punishment, while desiring the reward of the Ṣalāh to acquire a tranquil heart. Then one will have a peaceful soul and clear, balanced movements. So he focuses on all thoughts and actions, as well as what's mentioned in Ṣalāh from the beginning until the end, so as to make sure distracting thoughts and whims are not in the way. Thus khushu' is the spirit of Ṣalāh and the main point of it.

Alas, any Ṣalāh without khushu' is like a body without a soul in it.

KHUSHU' OF THE HEART

The foundation of the attention of the heart along with one's body parts is called khushu. When the heart has khushu', all parts of the body will have khushu'. That's why Sa'eed bin Musayb (raḍiallahu 'anhu) brought to attention that there was a man playing around in Ṣalāh. He said:

لَوْ خَشِعَ قَلْبُ هَذَا لَخَشِعَتْ جَوَارِحُهُ

"Had the heart of this person had khushu' his branches would be steady." (Sharh Al-Sunnah).

THE SHAYTAN AGAINST KHUSHU'

It is known by those with Khushu' that the worshiper of Allāh only receives the Ṣalāh in parts where attention of the heart exists. Shayṭān wants the slaves of Allāh to not pray so that they become from the abiders of the Hellfire. Whenever a person performs Ṣalāh, Shayṭān begins whispering to distract from the Ṣalāh, to make it null and void or at least less complete. In the Ḥadīth:

إِنَّ الْعَبْدَ لَيُصَلِّي الصَّلَاةَ لَا يَكْتُبُ لَهُ إِلَّا رُبْعُهَا، إِلَّا خُمْسَهَا، إِلَّا سُدسهَا، حَتَّى بَلَغَ عُشرهَا.

"The slave goes to pray a Ṣalāh and finds that only a quarter is safe or a fifth or a sixth all the way to only a tenth or a small percentage." (Narrated by Abū Dāwud Al-Nasa'ee and Ibn Hibban)

The Prophet Muḥammad (ﷺ) was merciful and generous to the 'Ummah. Therefore, he led them to the necessary weapon they needed to face the enemy Iblīs.

Once a person plans to go to the masjid or anywhere else he should say:

بِاسْمِ اللهِ ، آمَـنْـتُ بِاللهِ ، اعْـتَـصَـمْـتُ بِاللهِ ، تَـوَكَّـلْـتُ عَـلَـى اللهِ وَ لَا حَـوْلَ وَ قُـوَّةَ إِلَّا بِاللهِ .

"In the name of Allāh, I have faith in Allāh, protection is with Allāh, reliance is with Allāh, and there is no strength, might or power except with Allāh."

Whenever a person says this du'ā, it is said, "You have been guided, sufficed and protected." Then Shaytān leaves him alone.

Then by the time a person goes to the masjid he should be saying:

أَعُوذُ بِاللهِ الْـعَـظِـيـمِ وَ بِـوَجْـهِـهِ الْـكَـرِيـمِ وَ بِـسُـلْـطَـانِـهِ الْـقَـدِيـمِ مِـنَ الـشَّـيْـطَـانِ الـرَّجِـيـمِ .

'Audho billahi Al-'adheem wa bi-wajhe al-kareem wa besultani al-qadeem min al-shaytan al-rajeem

"I seek refuge in Allāh the Supreme and His Noble Face, along with His Everlasting Might from the outcast devil.

When a person says this duʿā, Shaytān whines:

عَصِمَ مِنِّي سَائِرَ الْيَوْم

"You have been protected from me the whole day." [Ḥadīth Ḥasan narrated by Abū Dawud with a good isnād]

During Ṣalāh, being content at heart, he says after the opening duʿā,

أَعُوذُ بِاللهِ السَّمِيعِ الْعَلِيمِ مِنَ الشَّيْطَانِ الرَّجِيمِ

'Audho billahi Al-Same' Al-'Aleem min Al-shaytan a-rajeem

"I seek refuge in Allāh, the All-Hearer, the Most Knowledgeable, from the outcast devil."

As a follower in the Ṣalāh, a person praying behind the Imām should be paying attention to what is being said and done. Especially when the recitation is out loud, he should listen to the

Table of Contents

TRANSLITERATION TABLE

Consonants

ء	ʾ	د	d	ض	ḍ	ك	k
ب	b	ذ	dh	ط	ṭ	ل	l
ت	t	ر	r	ظ	ẓ	م	m
ث	th	ز	z	ع	ʿ	ن	n
ج	j	س	s	غ	gh	هـ	h
ح	ḥ	ش	sh	ف	f	و	w
خ	kh	ص	ṣ	ق	q	ي	y

Vowels

Short	ـَ	a	ـِ	i	ـُ	u
Long	ـَا	ā	ـِي	ī	ـُو	ū

Diphthongs	ـَوْ	aw	ـَيْ	ay

Arabic Symbols & their meanings

حفظه الله	May Allāh preserve him
رَضِيَاللَّهُعَنْهُ	

May Allāh be pleased with him (i.e. a male companion of the Prophet Muḥammad)

سُبْحَانَهُ وَتَعَالَى   Glorified & Exalted is Allāh

عَزَّوَجَلَّ   (Allāh) the Mighty & Sublime

تَبَارَكَ وَتَعَالَى   (Allāh) the Blessed & Exalted

جَلَّ وَعَلَا   (Allāh) the Sublime & Exalted

عَلَيْهِ الصَّلَاةُ وَالسَّلَامُ   May Allāh send Blessings & Safety upon him (i.e. a Prophet or Messenger)

صَلَّى اللهُ عَلَيْهِ وَعَلَى آلِهِ وَسَلَّمَ   May Allāh send Blessings & Safety upon him and his family (i.e. Duʿāʾ sent when mentioning the Prophet Muḥammad)

رَحِمَهُ اللهُ   May Allāh have mercy upon him

رَضِيَ اللهُ عَنْهُمْ   May Allāh be pleased with them (i.e. Duʿāʾ made for the Companions of the Prophet Muḥammad)

جَلَّ جَلَالُهُ   (Allāh) His Majesty is Exalted

رَضِيَ اللهُ عَنْهَا   May Allāh be pleased with her (i.e. a female companion of the Prophet Muḥammad)

ATTENTION IN ṢALĀH, ATTENTIVENESS OF THE HEART, AND TREATING DISTRACTIONS

All praise belongs to Allāh. He whom made Ṣalāh a pillar of the religion and a strong connection between Allāh and His believing servants. Peace and blessings be upon Muhammad, the Trustworthy, his family, and all his Companions.

As to what follows:

Khushu' is tranquility through peace and humility along with uprightness, as Allāh, the Most High says:

$$\text{﴿ قَدْ أَفْلَحَ ٱلْمُؤْمِنُونَ ① ٱلَّذِينَ هُمْ فِي صَلَاتِهِمْ خَـٰشِعُونَ ② ﴾}$$

"Successful indeed are the believers. Those who offer their *Ṣalāt* (prayers) with all solemnity and full submissiveness."

." [*Sūrah al-Mu'minūn* 23:1-2]

Meaning, indeed this is victory and happiness for the believers who perform Ṣalāh. As some of their traits are **"Those who offer their Ṣalāh (prayers) with all solemnity and full submissiveness."**

Al-Khushu' **in Ṣalāh:** Presence of the heart therein before Allāh, the Most High, in love and honor, fearing His punishment, while desiring the reward of the Ṣalāh to acquire a tranquil heart. Then one will have a peaceful soul and clear, balanced movements. So he focuses on all thoughts and actions, as well as what's mentioned in Ṣalāh from the beginning until the end, so as to make sure distracting thoughts and whims are not in the way. Thus khushu' is the spirit of Ṣalāh and the main point of it.

Alas, any Ṣalāh without khushu' is like a body without a soul in it.

KHUSHU' OF THE HEART

The foundation of the attention of the heart along with one's body parts is called khushu. When the heart has khushu', all parts of the body will have khushu'. That's why Sa'eed bin Musayb (raḍiallahu 'anhu) brought to attention that there was a man playing around in Ṣalāh. He said:

لَوْ خَشِعَ قَلْبُ هَذَا لَخَشِعَتْ جَوَارِحُهُ

"Had the heart of this person had khushu' his branches would be steady." (Sharh Al-Sunnah).

THE SHAYTAN AGAINST KHUSHU'

It is known by those with Khushu' that the worshiper of Allāh only receives the Ṣalāh in parts where attention of the heart exists. Shayṭān wants the slaves of Allāh to not pray so that they become from the abiders of the Hellfire. Whenever a person performs Ṣalāh, Shayṭān begins whispering to distract from the Ṣalāh, to make it null and void or at least less complete. In the Ḥadīth:

إِنَّ الْعَبْدَ لَيُصَلِّي الصَّلَاةَ لَا يُكْتَبُ لَهُ إِلَّا رُبُعُهَا، إِلَّا خُمْسَهَا، إِلَّا سُدُسَهَا، حَتَّى بَلَغَ عُشْرَهَا.

"The slave goes to pray a Ṣalāh and finds that only a quarter is safe or a fifth or a sixth all the way to only a tenth or a small percentage." (Narrated by Abū Dāwud Al-Nasa'ee and Ibn Hibban)

The Prophet Muḥammad (ﷺ) was merciful and generous to the 'Ummah. Therefore, he led them to the necessary weapon they needed to face the enemy Iblīs.

Once a person plans to go to the masjid or anywhere else he should say:

بِاسْمِ اللهِ ، آمَنْتُ بِاللهِ ، اعْتَصَمْتُ بِاللهِ ، تَوَكَّلْتُ عَلَى اللهِ وَ لَا حَوْلَ وَ قُوَّةَ إِلَّا بِاللهِ.

"In the name of Allāh, I have faith in Allāh, protection is with Allāh, reliance is with Allāh, and there is no strength, might or power except with Allāh."

Whenever a person says this duʿā, it is said, "You have been guided, sufficed and protected." Then Shaytān leaves him alone.

Then by the time a person goes to the masjid he should be saying:

أَعُوذُ بِاللهِ الْعَظِيمِ وَ بِوَجْهِهِ الْكَرِيمِ وَ بِسُلْطَانِهِ الْقَدِيمِ مِنَ الشَّيْطَانِ الرَّجِيمِ.

'Audho billahi Al-'adheem wa bi-wajhe al-kareem wa besultani al-qadeem min al-shaytan al-rajeem

"I seek refuge in Allāh the Supreme and His Noble Face, along with His Everlasting Might from the outcast devil.

When a person says this du'ā, Shaytān whines:

عَصِمَ مِنّي سَائِرَ الْيَوْمِ

"You have been protected from me the whole day." [Ḥadīth Ḥasan narrated by Abū Dawud with a good isnād]

During Ṣalāh, being content at heart, he says after the opening du'ā,

أَعُوذُ بِاللهِ السَّمِيعِ الْعَلِيمِ مِنَ الشَّيْطَانِ الرَّجِيمِ

'Audho billahi Al-Same' Al-'Aleem min Al-shaytan a-rajeem

"I seek refuge in Allāh, the All-Hearer, the Most Knowledgeable, from the outcast devil."

As a follower in the Ṣalāh, a person praying behind the Imām should be paying attention to what is being said and done. Especially when the recitation is out loud, he should listen to the recitation. And when the Imām is quiet, those following should enter into recitation.

OUTWARD EXPRESSIONS OF KHUSHU'

From the expressions of khushu' in Ṣalāh: one hand over the left wrist while facing the place of prostration. Do not look up while in Ṣalāh nor look right nor left. Be keen not to play around or be disturbed by clothing, etc. Also, it is not proper to crack fingers or connect them during Ṣalāh. All of this negates khushu'. Ibn 'Abbās (raḍiallahu 'anhum) states:

$$رَكْعَتَانِ فِي تَفَكُّرٍ خَيْـرٌ مِنْ قِيَامِ لَيْـلَةٍ وَ الْـقَـلْـبُ سَاهٍ.$$

"Two rakah with reflection is better than staying the whole night in Ṣalāh with a heart that is inattentive." (Sharh Al-Sunnah)

Salman Al-Farisi (raḍiallahu anhu) said:

$$الـصَّـلَاةُ مِـكْـيَـالٌ فَـمَـنْ وَفَّى وُفِّـيَ لَـهُ، وَ مَـنْ طَـفَّـفَ فَـقَـدْ عَـلِـمْـتُـمْ مَا قَالَ اللهُ فِـي الْـمُـطَـفِّـفِـيـنَ.$$

"As-Ṣalāh measures in balance. Whoever is loyal and dutiful will be satisfied and treated as such. While the one who acts to

try to bring unbalance will be treated like those whom Allāh mentions in al-Muṭ affifīn."

Ḥadīth:

أَسْوَأُ النَّاسِ سُرْقَةُ الَّذِي يَسْرِقُ مِنْ صَلَاتِهِ

"Worst of all people are those that allow theft to happen from Ṣalāh."

Meaning, the one who does not complete rukū', nor sujūd' nor recitation in it. (Ahmad)

Ḥadīth:

إِنَّ اللهَ يَنْصِبُ وَجْهَهُ لِوَجْهِ عَبْدِهِ فِي صَلَاتِهِ مَا لَمْ يَلْتَفِتْ.

"Know that Allāh leads His Face to the face of the 'abd during Ṣalāh unless one allows himself to become distracted."

To be distracted is of two categories:

❖ The heart being distracted from Allāh, the Most High, to somebody else.

❖ The eyes being distracted from Ṣalāh.

Both of them are prohibited. Surely Allāh continues to be attentive towards His servant as long as one is attentive during Ṣalāh. Therefore, whenever a worshiper gives his attention to something else during the Ṣalāh Allāh is no longer required to give a reward.

The Prophet (ﷺ) was asked about this topic and explained it as,

هُوَ اِخْتِلَاسٌ يَخْتَلِسُهُ الـشَّيْطَانُ مِنْ صَلَاةِ الْعَبْدِ

"Sneaking and theft that the Shaytān engages in while the slave is trying to perform Ṣalāh."

In one narration it is said:

إِيَّاكَ وَ الْاِلْتِفَاتَ فِي الصَّلَاةِ فَإِنَّهَا هَلَكَةٌ

"Beware of inattentiveness in Ṣalāh as that itself is destructive." (al-Tirmidhī)

We see that when a person plans to stand before a leader or king, he or she will become externally ornamented and kempt, attentive in hearing and seeing as well. It makes more sense that a person entering Ṣalāh will provide more attention since

Allāh is aware of the servant's seeing and hearing. Allāh is the King of kings Who deserves all fear and love, humility and reverence. He knows the hopes, desires and fears of all. Thus, He knows the hidden and present. This means one should be more prepared.

As-Ṣalāh, with all its movements (i.e., bowing, prostration, and standing), means complete obedience and submissiveness to Allāh, the Lord of all that exists, by obeying His commands and not disobeying Him in all times and places.

LEVELS OF KHUSHU'

Imām ibn al-Qayyim (رَحِمَهُ ٱللَّهُ) said in his book, *al-Wābil al-Sayyib min al-Kalim at-Tayyib*:

People are placed into five levels with regards to the prayer:

1. The person who oppresses his/her soul through laxity. This is through weak performance in the pillars, wuḍū', Ṣalāh, its timings and limits.

2. The person who is okay with the wuḍū', pillars, and time/limits outwardly. Yet, the person is dealing with a waswas (whispering in Ṣalāh). Thus, they exit prayer without notice.

3. The one who prays properly. He or she is keen to observe the boundaries and pillars, performing jihad against the nafs and defending against waswas. This means the servant is busy in defending against the enemies who try to steal from his Ṣalāh. Thus, this category is in Ṣalāh and Jihād.

4. The person who perfects the rights of the Ṣalāh (as the Ṣalāh has duties). More than the

arkan/hudūd, the person is wholeheartedly immersed in it, focusing on what is required. Nay, their whole concern is in performing Ṣalāh according to the way it should be.

5. The person who also perfects the rights of Allāh and establishes the pillars and boundaries of the Ṣalāh. Facing Allāh, the prayer of this person is filled with the supremacy of Allāh and muraqabah (i.e., watching one's soul who wishes for Allāh). This person's Ṣalāh is more supreme than what's between the heaven and the earth.

The first is punished, the second is called to account, the third will have his shortcomings expiated due to his struggle, the fourth will be rewarded, and the fifth is brought close to his Rabb as He was given a source of reward in that the Ṣalāh is the calmness and coolness of his eyes. Thus, he or she is relaxed by the Ṣalāh. This is similar to when the Prophet (ﷺ) said:

أَرِحْـنَـا يَـا بِـلَالُ بِـالـصَّـلَاةِ

"Oh Bilāl let us relax by praying" [Zād Al-Ma'ād]

And he said:

جعــلـت قُــرَّة عَـيْـنِـي فِي الــصّـلاةِ

"My eyes only find contentment in Ṣalāh."
[Al-Jāmi' Al-Ṣaghīr].

The person who finds contentment with Allāh will always be happy. The one whose eyes don't find contentment in Ṣalāh will see that the dunyā will be filled with sadness and discontentment. It will be for him woe upon woe.

The way a servant becomes filled with khushu' in Ṣalāh is that they overcome their lusts and keep busy with remembrance of their Lord. Otherwise, he or she will remain a heart that is a prisoner of lusts and desires and Shaytān finds within his or her soul a place to sit. Like it is said: the empty soul is the devil's playground. How after that will one be free from waswas and empty thoughts?

WAYS THAT THE ṢALĀH WILL BE ACCEPTED

Some scholars of Islām said that the Ṣalāh has to have four traits to be lifted to the skies in acceptance:

حُضُـورُ قَـلْبٍ، وَ شَـهُـودُ عَـقَـلٍ، وَ خُـضُـوعُ أَرْكَـانٍ، وَ خُـشُـوعُ الْـجَـوَارِج .

"Presence of the heart, intellect, adherence to the pillars and humility of oneself and the body."

The person who prays without the heart being present is fooling about. To pray without intellect is to be forgetful. To pray without the pillars is to have a lack of adherence. Whoever has a prayer with these four qualities is a loyal person who is properly subservient.

The Messenger of Allāh (ﷺ) instructed us that if we pray a prayer to make it perfect as if it is our last pray thus he said:

صَـلِّ صَـلَاةَ مـودِع

"Pray as though it is your farewell prayer."

A farewell prayer meaning as if it is the last prayer you will pray in your life.

AL-KHUSHU' AND DHIKR OF ALLĀH

Khushu' in Ṣalāh is a condition ensuring that the outward body parts find tranquility through the actions of Ṣalāh. Along with that, adhkar are pronounced, said with a present and sane mind. Reflection and what is needed for that to happen occurs. Daily engagements noticed by the heart are a result of honoring Allah and holding Allāh dear to the heart. Also, having feelings directed to Him by the heart in humbleness and a long supplication' called Qunūt. Ṣalāh is not completed with khushu' unless there is reason. Even if the physical expressions of the Sunnah are present or spoken, the Ṣalāh without khushu' is not satisfactory.

And khushu' is not realized except by those who concern themselves with purifying the soul by consistent dhikr by the heart and tongue. Remind your heart to be softened by remembering Allāh on your tongue. Then one may be blessed to find a hard heart that has been uplifted spiritually. It is through certainty in 'Īmān that a person may perform the worship of Allāh as if the heart truly acknowledges and sees Allāh. Allāh says,

$$﴿ * أَلَمْ يَأْنِ لِلَّذِينَ ءَامَنُوٓا۟ أَن تَخْشَعَ قُلُوبُهُمْ لِذِكْرِ ٱللَّهِ وَمَا نَزَلَ مِنَ ٱلْحَقِّ ﴾$$

"Has not the time come for the hearts of those who believe (in the Oneness of Allah - Islamic Monotheism) to be affected by Allah's Reminder (this Qur'ān), and that which has been revealed of the truth." [*Sūrah al-Hadīd* 57:16]

Excellency ('Ihsān) was explained by the Prophet (صَلَّى ٱللَّهُ عَلَيْهِ وَسَلَّمَ) as:

$$الْإِحْسَانُ بِأَنْ تَعْبُدَ اللهَ كَأَنَّكَ تَرَاهُ فَإِنْ لَمْ تَكُنْ تَرَاهُ فَإِنَّهُ يَرَاكَ .$$

"To worship Allāh as if you see him, and though you do not see Him, then know that He sees you."

AL-KHUSHU' & THE HEART

What is referred to as Khushu'?

Between acquiring many different meanings that are directed to Allāh by one being attached to none else. Thus, one recognizes and honors Allāh and His supremeness. Humbling oneself towards Him and achieving an admirable tranquility to face only Him. One must hold this serious feeling of completeness in every word and action. This is done during the Ṣalāh. Thus, khushu' is when the heart is uplifted in reverence to the Lord.

Those who have reached a higher level of worship and knowledge have agreed that khushu' is located in the heart. Its fruit is realized on the limbs. The Khashi' is the one who has reverence to Allāh and is fearful of Allāh. The explanation of khushu' in Ṣalāh is to gather concentration for it and ignore all else.

This khushu' is how one enhances the skill of observed psychological limits. This, of course, is one of the major causes of success in traits of this life.

And He related successfulness of those in Ṣalāh with khushu' in the Muslim's Ṣalāh. As we can now conclude that he who has no khushu' in his Ṣalāh, then he is not from the people of success.

From that which ruins Ṣalāh is intentional speech, laughter, eating, and drinking, exposing ones 'awrah or turning away from the Qiblah, fidgeting too much or excreting najasah. As for that which protects from Shaytān is to seek refuge in Allāh in order to reject him. Also, to be certain in rejecting Shaytān along with dhikr of Allāh the Most High. He (ﷺ):

رَأَيْتُ رَجُلاً مِنْ أُمَّتِي قَدِ احْتَوشَتْهُ الشَّيَاطِينَ فَجَاءَ ذِكْرُ اللهِ فَطرد الشَّيْطَانُ عَنْهُ.

"I saw a man from my Ummah that Shaytān had caused to become lonely and empty. Then came dhikr of Allāh which removed and rejected Shaytān from him." {al-Wabel al-Sayyeb}

My brother Muslim: Preserve your Ṣalāh with its' conditions, pillars, compulsory and khushu' tradition, and completion in order that Allāh will protect you from it. We are aware that the Prophet

(صَلَّاللَّهُعَلَيْهِوَسَلَّمَ) gave the comparison of Ṣalāh with a flowing river that one bathes in 5 times every single day. So that the dirtiness and unwholesomeness leaves. Saying:

فَكَذَلِكَ الـصَّـلَـوَاتُ الـخَـمْـسُ يَـمْـحُـو اللهُ بِـهِـنَّ الـخَـطَـايَـا .

"Such is the five Ṣalāh by which Allāh removes one's sins and faults." (Agreed upon)

Allāh (سُبْحَانَهُوَتَعَالَى) says,

﴿ وَٱلَّذِينَ هُمْ عَلَىٰ صَلَاتِهِمْ يُحَافِظُونَ ۝ أُوْلَٰٓئِكَ فِى جَنَّٰتٍ مُّكْرَمُونَ ۝ ﴾

"And those who guard their Ṣalāt (prayers) well, such shall dwell in the Gardens (i.e. Paradise) honored."" [Sūrah Al-Ma'arij 70:34- 35]

May Allāh make us and all Muslims amongst those who are attentive at their worshiping as those will dwell in Gardens honored. May He send plenty of prayers upon Muḥammad, his household and Companions. Sending many greetings.

PRACTICAL STEPS TO SUPPORT KHUSHU IN ṢALĀH

All praise belongs to Allāh Who made Ṣalāh the main aspect of the dīn, as He said:

﴿ وَإِنَّهَا لَكَبِيرَةٌ إِلَّا عَلَى ٱلْخَٰشِعِينَ ۝ ٱلَّذِينَ يَظُنُّونَ أَنَّهُم مُّلَٰقُوا۟ رَبِّهِمْ وَأَنَّهُمْ إِلَيْهِ رَٰجِعُونَ ۝ ﴾

"Truly it is extremely heavy and hard except for *Al-Khashi'un* [i.e. the true believers in Allāh - those who obey Allāh with full submission, fear much from His Punishment, and believe in His Promise (Paradise, etc.) and in His Warnings (Hell, etc.)]. (They are those) who are certain that they are going to meet their Lord, and that unto Him they are going to return." [*Sūrah al-Baqarah* 2:45-46]

May Allāh send peace and blessings on our noble Prophet Muḥammad since it is clear in the seerah that the Ṣalāh was the most important thing to us as an 'Ummah.

AL-KHUSHU'
IT'S SIGNIFICANCE AND EFFECTS

There is a dilemma which was present upon many. Harshness in the heart, lack of tears and a nearly non-existent reflection on the Qur'ān and the Sunnah and life. All of this is due to a consistent presence of sway or a consistent lack of principle that overcomes our hearts. It is like a crossroad has led us to take the path of lacking khushu', even in our actions of worship, which makes it very difficult for our hearts to retain khushu' after this poor state of events has taken place.

It takes the Ṣaḥābah like ʿUthmān ibn Affān (رَضِيَ ٱللَّهُ عَنْهُ) to explain:

لَوْ طَهَرَتْ قُلُوبُكُمْ مَا شَبِعْتُمْ مِنْ كَلَامِ اللهِ عَزَّ وَ جَلَّ.

"Had your hearts been pure, then you would never reach full from the completeness of the words of Allāh." (al-Zuhd of Imām Ahmad)

Al-Imām ibn Qayyim, referring to khushu' al-'Īmān, says:

خُشُـوعُ الْـقَـلْـبِ لله بِالتَّعْظِيمِ وَ الْإِجْـلَالِ وَ الْـوقَارِ وَ الْـمَـهَـابَـةِ وَ الْـحَـيَـاءِ، فَـيَـنْكَـسِرُ الْـقَـلْـبُ لله كَـسْـرَةً مُـمْـتَـلِـئَـةً مِـنَ الْـوَجِلِ وَ الْـخـجِلِ وَ الْـحُبِّ وَ الْـحَـيَـاءِ، وَ شُـهُـود نِعَـم اللهِ ، وَ جَـنَـايَـاتُـهُ هُـوَ فَـيَـخْـشَـعُ الْـقَـلْـب لَا مَـحَـالَـةَ فَـيَـتْـبَـعُـهُ خُـشُـوعُ الْـجَـوَارِج .

"Khushu' of the qalb (heart) to Allāh, with expressing supremacy, honor, sensitivity and exposure thus such one will express a turned and open heart. This open heart is one filled with purity, love, and serenity. To witness the blessings of Allāh and one's crimes in lieu of this. Khushu' enters the heart in no other way. And khushu' of the limbs follows." (Al-Ruh ibn Qayyim)

Amongst the aspects that show that khushu' is the deciding factor in the acceptance of Ṣalāh is that it is the most important pillar after the testimony of faith.

It is mentioned in the Sunan of the Prophet (ﷺ) that he said:

إِنَّ الْعَبْدَ لَيَنْصَرِفُ مِنْ صَلَاتِهِ، وَ لَمْ يَكْتُبْ لَـهُ مِنْهَا إِلَّا نِصْفُهَا، إِلَّا ثُلُثهَا، إِلَّا رُبَعهَا، إِلَّا خُمسهَا، إِلَّا سُدُسهَا، إِلَّا سبعهَا، إِلَّا ثمنهَا، تسعهَا، إِلَّا عشرهَا.

"Verily, the servant of Allāh leaves from Ṣalāh without having written in it even a half, nor a third, nor a fourth, nor a sixth, nor one-seventh, until one reaches after an eighth and a ninth just a tenth of it."

Meaning, slowly one gains less and less of the Ṣalāh all due to khushu'. On the other hand, khushu' is fulfilling and eases the love one has for Ṣalāh. Shaykh ʿAbdur Raḥmān al-Saʿdī says in his tafsīr (of the verse):

"And it is difficult except for al-Khashi'īn"

Meaning, those who are humble in Ṣalāh, it becomes easy and light for them, as khushu' and fear of Allāh and hope for what is with Allāh allows for the performing of the Ṣalāh with ease in one's chest. Due to the attention is given to reward and fear which has in punishment. Likewise, khushu' is true knowledge.[1]

Ibn Rajab (رَحِمَهُ ٱللَّهُ) explains the Ḥadīth of Abī Ad-Dardāʾ regarding the virtue of knowledge. From ʿUbadah ibn Al-Samit and ʿAwf ibn Malik along with Ḥudhayfah (رَضِيَ ٱللَّهُ عَنْهُمْ) that they said:

أَوَّلُ عِلْمٍ يُرْفَعُ مِنَ النَّاسِ الْخُشُوعُ حَتَّى لَا تَرَى خَاشِعاً.

"The first knowledge to be lifted from the people is al-khushu' thus you won't see any individual who has any khashi'."

Other Ḥadīth show that the departure of knowledge is due to the departure of action. The Companions (رَضِيَ ٱللَّهُ عَنْهُمْ) held the tafsīr as internal knowledge escaping from the hearts. And that is khushu'. These are authentic narrations.

So Ṣalāh is a connection between the servant and his Lord. Hence a person cuts off from all other distractions in life. The individual turns with his or her whole human self to the Lord (i.e., Allāh) in order to achieve guidance and support. What can

---

[1]Tafsīr Saʿdī

explain this is achieving wholeness once (due to the Ṣalāh). Now one should ask to be fully on the way of the Straight Path.

People are differential in this connection. For example, some people after this Ṣalāh are more gathering on the path of Allāh. Others do not achieve anything in particular at all. So their Ṣalāh is seen with reading out loud and movements, dhikr and tasbīh, but it is without any feeling to what's being done or said.

Due to this, one should keep in mind that Ṣalāh is not words one has on his tongue or movements that one holds to perform on limbs if there is no taddabur (reflection) from the intellect or khushu' of the heart.

From Abū Hurayrah (رَضِيَ اللّٰهُ عَنْهُ) in Sunan al-Tirmidhī:

إِنَّ أَوَّلَ مَا يُحَاسَبُ بِهِ الْعَبْدُ يَوْمَ الْقِيَامَةِ مِنْ عَمَلِهِ الصَّلَاةُ، فَإِنْ صَلُحَتْ فَقَدْ أَفْلَحَ وَ أَنْجَحَ، وَ إِنْ فَسَدَتْ فَقَدْ خَابَ وَ خَسِرَ فَإِنْ انْتَقَصَ مِنْ فَرِيضَتِهِ شَيْئاً قَالَ الرَّبُّ عَزَّ وَ جَلَّ: اُنْظُرُواْ هَلْ لِعَبْدِي مِنْ تَطَوَّعٍ! فَيُكْمِلُ

بِهَا مَا انْتَقَصَ مِنَ الْفَرِيضَةِ ثُمَّ تَكُونُ سَائِرُ
أَعْمَالِهِ عَلَى هَذَا.

"The first deeds that the servant will be brought to account for is Ṣalāh. If that is sound, then the rest will be accepted and he will succeed. If it is not sound, then he will be lost as the obligatory aspects of Ṣalāh are diminished. Then the Lord will say: "Look to see if my servant has any voluntary deeds. This voluntary deeds will complete the fareedah along with all deeds according to this way."

When we noticed that a lot of people lack khushu' in Ṣalāh, it became necessary to go over the ways to return to the pure Ṣalāh that has fulfillment and re-connect with Allāh with Ṣalāh of the whole heart and limbs. Allāh praised those with this character amongst the believers,

﴿ قَدْ أَفْلَحَ ٱلْمُؤْمِنُونَ ۝ ٱلَّذِينَ هُمْ فِي صَلَاتِهِمْ خَٰشِعُونَ ۝ ﴾

"Successful indeed are the believers. Those who offer their Ṣalāt (prayers) with all solemnity and full submissiveness." [Sūrah Al-Mu'minūn 23:1:2]

Perhaps we will understand the ayah where Allāh says:

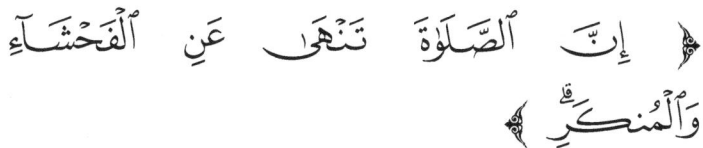

"Verily, *As-Ṣalāh* (the prayer) prevents from *Al-Fahsha'* (i.e. great sins of every kind, unlawful sexual intercourse, etc.) and *Al-Munkar* (i.e. disbelief, polytheism, and every kind of evil wicked deed, etc.)" [*Sūrah Al-Ankabut* 29: 45]

We need to ask ourselves what is the matter with many of us who leave from praying and then commit evil acts. There is a big difference between it and what is left from the prayer of those who have khushu' and those who often return in repentance (i.e., to Allāh) in which the effect of their prayer upon the one who performs it. So the one of them who leaves from praying feels with every prayer as though his heart has been cleansed from the filth of this worldly life and has come closer to Allāh (عَزَّوَجَلَّ).

MEANS FOR ATTAINING KHUSHU'

It is inevitable that there are things that diminish one's khushu' and no doubt there are mistakes and flaws in our performance of the Ṣalāh. Perhaps in this talk, by Allāh's permission, we can explore some helpful guidelines towards having khushu' in the Ṣalāh. They are:

Having true ʾĪmān and a firm creed (i.e., belief):

Having true ʾĪmān and a firm creed is what results in having khushu'. This a tremendous virtue in this life and in the Hereafter. Also, having awareness (i.e., in the Ṣalāh) coupled with calmness, tranquility, and ease has no equivalent or sweetness that can be surpassed.

Allāh (سُبْحَانَهُوَتَعَالَى) says,

$$ \text{﴿ قَدْ أَفْلَحَ ٱلْمُؤْمِنُونَ ۝ ٱلَّذِينَ هُمْ فِى صَلَاتِهِمْ خَٰشِعُونَ ۝ ﴾} $$

"Successful indeed are the believers. Those who offer their *Ṣalāh* (prayers) with all solemnity and full submissiveness." [*Sūrah Al-Mu'minūn* 23:1-2]

Imām Muslim narrated on the authority of 'Uthmān bin Affān (رَضِىَ ٱللَّهُ عَنْهُ) that he said, "I heard the Messenger of Allāh (صَلَّى ٱللَّهُ عَلَيْهِ وَسَلَّمَ) say,

مَا مِنِ امْرِئٍ مُسْلِمٍ تَحْضُرُهُ صَلَاةٌ مَكْتُوبَةٌ فَيُحْسِنُ وُضُوءَهَا وَخُشُوعَهَا وَرُكُوعَهَا إِلَّا كَانَتْ كَفَّارَةً لِمَا قَبْلَهَا مِنَ الذُّنُوبِ مَا لَمْ يُؤْتِ كَبِيرَةً وَذَلِكَ الدَّهْرَ كُلَّهُ

"When the time for a prescribed prayer comes, if any Muslim performs ablution well and offers his prayer with humility and bowing, it will be an expiation for his past sins, so long as he has not committed a major sin; and this applies for all times."

The verses and aḥadīth that attest to the virtue of khushu are numerous.

STRIVING TO PERFORM LENGTHY RECITATION AND DHIKR

To recite a lot and have lots of dhikr which entails seeking Allāh's forgiveness as opposed to too much talkativeness.

لَا تَكْثُرُوا الْكَلَامَ بَغَيْرِ ذِكْرِ اللهِ: فَإِنَّ كَثْرَةَ الْكَلَامِ بَغَيْرِ ذِكْرِ تَعَالَى قَسْوَةٌ لِلْقَلْبِ! وَ إِنَّ أَبْعَدَ النَّاسِ مِنَ اللهِ الْقَلْبُ الْقَاسِي.

"Do not talk too much! Talking too much instead of dhikr of Allāh will harden the heart. The farthest person from Allāh is the hard heart." [Collected by At-Tirmidhī]

Recitation of the Qur'ān and reflecting on its verses are from the closest ways to make the heart soft.

﴿ اللَّهُ نَزَّلَ أَحْسَنَ الْحَدِيثِ كِتَابًا مُتَشَابِهًا مَثَانِيَ تَقْشَعِرُّ مِنْهُ جُلُودُ الَّذِينَ يَخْشَوْنَ رَبَّهُمْ ثُمَّ تَلِينُ جُلُودُهُمْ وَقُلُوبُهُمْ إِلَى ذِكْرِ اللَّهِ ﴾

"Allah has sent down the best statement, a Book (this Qur'ān), its parts resembling each other in goodness and truth, oft-

repeated. The skins of those who fear their Lord shiver from it (when they recite it or hear it). Then their skin and their heart soften to the remembrance of Allah." [*Sūrah Az-Zumar* 39:23]

Recitation and dhikr are a protection and shield from Shayṭān and his whispers. They are also a way to comfort the heart. This is something that is lost on many people.

﴿ ٱلَّذِينَ ءَامَنُواْ وَتَطۡمَئِنُّ قُلُوبُهُم بِذِكۡرِ ٱللَّهِ أَلَا بِذِكۡرِ ٱللَّهِ تَطۡمَئِنُّ ٱلۡقُلُوبُ ۝ ﴾

"Those who believe (in the Oneness of Allāh - Islamic Monotheism), and whose hearts find rest in the remembrance of Allah, Verily, in the remembrance of Allāh do hearts find rest." [*Sūrah Ar-Rad* 13: 28]

Also, dhikr of Allāh (عَزَّوَجَلَّ) is a means to success.

﴿ وَٱذۡكُرُواْ ٱللَّهَ كَثِيرًا لَّعَلَّكُمۡ تُفۡلِحُونَ ۝ ﴾

"And remember Allāh much, that you may be successful." [*Sūrah Al-Jumu'ah* 62:10]

Now the reader knows that that dhikr is from the ways to increase in khushu'. Thus, the one who wants more knowledge about the virtue of dhikr should return to the Book of Allāh and the numerous dhikr exemplified by the Prophet (صَلَّى ٱللَّهُ عَلَيْهِ وَسَلَّمَ).

Performing jihad against Shaytān before entering Ṣalāh helps as well as it is a way of holding onto determination before standing to perform Ṣalāh. If the Shaytān tries to distract you in the beginning of Ṣalāh, one should not surrender in the middle of Ṣalāh until the end and then at the last moment strive to reach the highest point in one's Ṣalāh.

Shaytān tries to distract the mind, so the one praying doesn't understand anything from his Ṣalāh. Imām Muslim narrated on the authority of 'Uthmān ibn Abī Al-Aas (رَضِيَ ٱللَّهُ عَنْهُ) that he said:

يَا رَسُولَ اللهِ، إِنَّ الشَّيْطَانَ حَالَ بَيْنِي وَ بَيْنَ صَلَاتِي وَ بَيْنَ قِرَاءَتِي يَلبِسُهَا عَلَيَّ، فَقَالَ رَسُولُ اللهِ صَلَّى اللهُ عَلَيْهِ وَ سَلَّمَ: ذَاكَ شَيْطَانٌ يُقَالُ لَهُ خِنْزِبٌ، فَإِذَا أَحْسَسْتَهُ فَتَعَوَّذْ بِاللهِ وَاتفِلْ عَنْ يَسَارِكَ ثَلَاثاً.

"Oh Messenger of Allāh, no doubt Shayṭān stands between me and my Ṣalāh and when I recite Shaytān disturbs me. The Prophet (ﷺ) said: "That is a Shaytān named Khinzab. If you are interrupted, then seek refuge in Allāh and blow with a little saliva to the left three times."

The one who narrated the Ḥadīth said,

"I did this so Allāh removed the disturbance."

Then, it is suitable that the one in Ṣalāh strives and adheres to the Ṣalāh properly. Seeing that if one's Ṣalāh was not performed properly that the next one should be. And if one notices the khushu' was less in one Ṣalāh, then the next one should have more khushu'.

The important point is not to give up hope in performing Ṣalāh. Also to ask Allāh's help in this by saying:

CONSTANT ACCOUNTABILITY AND WATCHFULNESS

Accounting and censuring oneself for what's not suitable in speech and action nor iʿtiqād.

﴿ يَٰٓأَيُّهَا ٱلَّذِينَ ءَامَنُوا۟ ٱتَّقُوا۟ ٱللَّهَ وَلْتَنظُرْ نَفْسٌ مَّا قَدَّمَتْ لِغَدٍ وَٱتَّقُوا۟ ٱللَّهَ إِنَّ ٱللَّهَ خَبِيرٌۢ بِمَا تَعْمَلُونَ ﴾ ﴿١٨﴾

"O you who believe! Fear Allāh and keep your duty to Him. And let every person look to what he has sent forth for the morrow, and fear Allāh. Verily, Allāh is All-Aware of what you do." [*Sūrah Al-Hashr* 59:18]

The leader of the believers, ʿUmar ibn Al-Khaṭṭāb (رَضِيَٱللَّهُعَنْهُ) said:

حَاسِبُوا أَنْفُسَكُمْ قَبْلَ أَنْ تُحَاسَبُوا، وَ زَنُوا أَنْفُسَكُمْ قَبْلَ أَنْ تُوزَنُوا، وَ تَزَيَّنُوا لِلْعَرْضِ الْأَكْبَرِ.

"Hold yourself to account before you are held accountable; and weigh your deeds

before they are weighed for you; and adorn yourself (i.e., with good deeds) for the biggest presentation (i.e., on the Day of Judgement)."

Likewise, stay away from acts of disobedience. So don't involve yourself in looking and what is haram. Keeping the tongue and hearing safe as far away from the haram as possible. This applies for all body parts. Instead, involve them with the servitude of Allāh. Attend to the Book of Allāh and beneficial books of knowledge, along with that which is permissible and reflect about His great creations. Allow oneself to enjoy the wholesome from words and beneficial speech. Its well-known that sins chain a person and block him from performing acts of worship in a suitable fashion. Every person knows their own sin more than others. Rectifying one's condition is more important. This is related with accounting oneself in order to find what rectifies.

Tadabbur Al-Qur'ān and Dhikr

Tadabbur means to reflect and tafahhum means to comprehend what is said in Ṣalāh. Not to pay attention to other than the point of sujūd. Feeling the search and awe in the situation when facing Allāh.

Ibn Qayyim mentions in the book Al-Fawā'id:

"A worshipper faces to statuses, to stand before Allāh in Ṣalāh and to stand before Allāh on the Day of Judgement. Giving due diligence at the beginning means the next stance will be easy. But the one that doesn't give attention in standing in Ṣalāh at the beginning will face hardship in the hereafter."

Allāh (سُبْحَانَهُوَتَعَالَى) says:

$$\text{﴿ وَمِنَ ٱلَّيْلِ فَٱسْجُدْ لَهُۥ وَسَبِّحْهُ لَيْلًا طَوِيلًا ۝ ﴾}$$

"And during the night, prostrate yourself to Him (i.e. the offering of *Maghrib* and *'Isha'* prayers), and glorify Him a long night through (i.e. *Tahajjud* prayer). Verily! These (disbelievers) love the present life of this world, and put behind them a heavy Day (that will be hard)." [*Sūrah Al-Insān* 76:26-27]

The prayer of a person who prays a final prayer will certainly contain what the prayer requires.

Imām Ahmad narrates on the authority of Abū Ayūb Al-Ansari (رَضِيَاللَّهُعَنْهُ) that a man came to the Prophet (صَلَّىاللَّهُعَلَيْهِوَسَلَّمَ) and said, "Give me a sermon that's concise." He (عَلَيْهِالصَّلَاةُوَالسَّلَامُ) said:

إِذَا قُمْتَ فِي صَلَاتِكَ فَصَلِّ صَلَاةَ مُوَدِّعٍ وَلاَ تَكَلَّمْ بِكَلَامٍ تَعْتَذِرُ مِنْهُ وَأَجْمِعِ الْيَأْسَ عَمَّا فِي أَيْدِي النَّاسِ

"When you stand to pray, pray like a man bidding farewell. Do not say anything for which you will have to apologize. And give up hope for what other people have."

There are other ways to reach khushu'. We mention amongst them.

Resilience and presence of the heart:

It is known that when you're concerned about a matter, then your heart will be present unconditionally. Thus, there is no way to treat this except by entering into Ṣalāh with a present heart. Inattentiveness is present in those who have less

'Īmān and are attached to the lowly life of this dunya and vice versa.

Seeking pleasure through Ṣalāh

The sweetness that the people of Ṣalāh find in themselves is what was described by Ibn Taymiyyah (رَحِمَهُ ٱللَّهُ) by saying:

"In the dunya is a Jannah, whoever doesn't enter it in the dunya won't enter Jannah in the Hereafter."

It is unbelievable that the Muslim finds this sweetness without care.

And this sweetness like what Ibn Qayyim describes is strengthened by how much love one has and weakened by how weak one becomes. Thus, it is benefitting that the Muslim paces along the way that leads to the love of Allāh."

Hastening to the Ṣalāh:

This is achieved by preparing the heart to stand before Allāh, the Mighty and Honorable. It is suitable to come early for Ṣalāh in order to recite what is easy along with reflection and humility. That is more likely to achieve khushu' in Ṣalāh.

In a Ḥadīth narrated by Bukhārī and Muslim from Abū Hurayrah (ﷺ):

لَوْ يَعْلَمُ النَّاسُ مَا فِي النَّدَاءِ وَالصَّفِّ الأَوَّلِ ثُمَّ لَمْ يَجِدُوا إِلاَّ أَنْ يَسْتَهِمُوا عَلَيْهِ لاَسْتَهَمُوا وَلَوْ يَعْلَمُونَ مَا فِي التَّهْجِيرِ لاَسْتَبَقُوا إِلَيْهِ

"If people knew what was in the adhan and the first row of the prayer and could only draw lots for it, they would draw lots. And if they knew what was in doing Dhuhr early, they would race each other to it."

Different is the gathering of the people of dunya compared to the gathering of the people of the Hereafter who read the Book of Allāh. Of course, the second group of people will be more virtuous in   Ṣalāh.

Having   haya'   (shyness)   of   Allāh:

For the worshipper to avoid being seen by the Mighty and Honorable in empty actions, void of any spirit, the feeling of shyness before Allāh pushes a Muslim to perfect his 'ibādah (i.e., worship). Likewise, the person will seek closeness to Allāh with Ṣalāh that encompasses sanctified feelings of fear and desire.

Observing the condition of the Salaf (pious ones who came before):

For the Muslim to observe the condition of the Companions and Salaf in Ṣalāh.

Ibn Taymiyyah (رحمه الله)- Muslim bin Yassir (radhiallahu anhu) used to pray in the masjid which was destroyed partially so the people left and he was in Ṣalāh not noticing anything else.

Then came war equipment against Abdullah bin Zubair and he was in Ṣalāh not noticing anything else.

They said to Amar ibn Al-Qays:

"'Does your self-consciousness distract you in Ṣalāh?' He answered: 'Is there anything more beloved to me than Ṣalāh?' They informed him that they have things that distract them in Ṣalāh."

He asked if it was with Hūr al-ʿīn and Jannah. He was then told that it was rather due to their wealth and families. He found that his whole life he never wanted that to happen.

These were some of the means to support khushu'- by the permission of Allāh. Therefore, we ask Allāh to support us in His obedience in the way that will keep Him pleased with us.

Made in the USA
Columbia, SC
30 April 2024

34829066R00031